World Book's Learning Ladders

Tough Trucks

WORLD BOOK

a Scott Fetzer company
Chicago
www.worldbookonline.com

World Book, Inc.
180 North LaSalle Street
Suite 900
Chicago, Illinois 60601
USA

For information about other World Book publications, visit our website at **http://www.worldbook.com** or call **1-800-WORLDBK (967-5325)**.

For information about sales to schools and libraries, call **1-800-975-3250 (United States); 1-800-837-5365 (Canada)**.

2008 revised printing

Library of Congress Cataloging-in-Publication Data

Tough trucks.
    p. cm. -- (World Book's learning ladders)
    Summary: "Introduction to heavy-duty trucks such as cranes, fire engines, tractors, and others, using simple text, question and answer format, illustrations, and photos. Features include puzzles and games, fun facts, resource list, and index"--Provided by publisher.
    Includes bibliographical references and index.
    ISBN 978-0-7166-7730-7
    1. Trucks--Juvenile literature.   I. World Book, Inc.
    TL230.15.T76 2007
    629.225--dc22
                        2007019914

World Book's Learning Ladders
Set ISBN: 978-0-7166-7725-3 (print)

E-book editions:
ISBN 978-0-7166-7764-2 (Learning Hub)
ISBN 978-0-7166-7765-9 (Spindle)
ISBN 978-0-7166-7766-6 (EPUB3)
ISBN 978-0-7166-7767-3 (PDF)

Printed in China by Shenzhen Wing King Tong Paper Products Co, Ltd., Shenzhen, Guangdong
9th printing June 2016

Editor in Chief: Paul A. Kobasa

Supplementary Publications
  Associate Director: Scott Thomas
  Managing Editor: Barbara A. Mayes

Senior Editor: Shawn Brennan

Editor: Dawn Krajcik

Researcher: Cheryl Graham

Manager, Contracts & Compliance
  (Rights & Permissions): Loranne K. Shields

Graphics and Design
  Associate Director: Sandra M. Dyrlund
  Associate Manager, Design: Brenda B. Tropinski
  Associate Manager, Photography: Tom Evans

Production
  Director, Manufacturing and Pre-Press: Carma Fazio
  Manager, Manufacturing: Steven Hueppchen
  Production Technology Manager: Anne Fritzinger
  Proofreader: Emilie Schrage

This edition is an adaptation of the Ladders series published originally by T&N Children's Publishing, Inc., of Minnetonka, Minnesota.

Photographic credits: Cover: © Francois Etienne du Plessis, Shutterstock; p7: Images Colour Library; p9: Robert Harding; p11: Telegraph Colour Library; p16: The Stock Market; p19: Still Pictures; p22: Britstock.

Illustrators: Gaëtan Evrard, Jon Stuart

What's inside?

This book tells you about different kinds of tough trucks. You can find out how people use these trucks to build tall buildings, put out fires, and clear away snow.

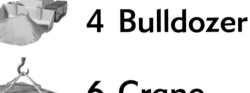

Bulldozer

A bulldozer is the first truck to arrive at a construction site. This tough truck pushes huge piles of rocks and dirt out of the way. It clears the ground quickly, so people can build new roads and houses.

The **cab** has thick windows to protect the driver from the noise of the clattering engine.

A bulldozer's sharp **prongs** break up hard, rocky ground.

Caterpillar tracks roll easily over the rocks and soil.

Smoke from the engine puffs out of a long **exhaust pipe**.

It's a fact!

This bulldozer works underwater! It is clearing a ditch so that pipes can be laid.

A metal **blade** pushes the heavy piles of rocks and dirt out of the way.

5

Crane

A crane lifts a heavy object high above your head. The crane can turn and reach and put the object in a different place. It can put a pipe into a deep hole or on top of a tall building!

This crane is lifting a big pipe that is hanging from wires. A **hook** grips the wires firmly.

A pipe is a heavy **load**.

It's a fact!

A crane lifts objects with its long arm. This crane's arm can stretch across a football field!

A crane's arm is called a **boom**. The boom can move up and down and from side to side, and it can stretch near or far.

A **crane driver** works the boom.

Tall cranes stand in a line at this busy port. They lift big boxes onto and off of ships.

Giant feet, called **jacks**, stop the crane from toppling over.

Cement mixer

A cement mixer delivers thick, wet concrete to a construction site. Inside the big drum, cement and other ingredients are mixed together to make concrete. The concrete is poured. After a while, it becomes hard and strong. Concrete is used to make walls, floors, roofs, and even bridges and highways.

Water for making the concrete is stored in a small **tank**.

It's a fact!

The drums of some cement mixers are big enough to hold a car.

The **drum** turns slowly to mix the sand, water, crushed rock, and powdery cement.

This mixer pumps its concrete high up to help finish building a new house.

The wet concrete slides down a **chute** to the ground.

A construction worker smooths the **concrete**. Soon, it will dry as hard as rock!

Excavator

An excavator picks up dirt and digs big holes. It's like a giant bucket and shovel. It scoops up dirt and moves it from one place to another.

It's a fact!

It would take one person 100 days to move as much dirt as an excavator can move in one hour.

Metal teeth cut into the rocky ground.

A large, heavy pile of soil and rocks can be scooped into the **bucket**.

A **turntable** lets the cab turn in a circle. The driver can pick up dirt in one place and then turn and dump it in another.

A long metal **arm** moves the bucket to where the driver wants to dig. The arm bends just like your arm does.

This excavator is emptying its bucket into a dump truck.

The driver pulls a **lever** to lift the bucket.

Construction site

Clatter, bang, whir!
The construction site is full
of trucks! What do
you think they
are building?

12

Words you know

Here are some words that you read earlier in this book. Say them out loud, then try to find the things in the picture.

chute
bucket
caterpillar tracks

jacks
boom
drum

Snowplow

When lots of snow falls, it can block busy roads and railroad tracks. It may even stop you from going to school! A snowplow makes a path through the deep snow so that traffic can move safely again.

A long **funnel** blows the snow far away from the road.

Some snowplows have **blades** that spin around and around. They pull the snow out of the drifts and into the blower.

Some snowplows have one huge, curved blade. The blade pushes the snow to the side of the road.

Windshield wipers quickly brush falling snow off of the driver's window.

It's a fact!

Snowplows are put on the front of trains to help clear piles of snow off railroad tracks.

Bright **headlights** help the driver to see ahead.

Strong **chains** grip the slippery road. They stop the wheels from skidding.

Garbage truck

When you throw something away, it ends up in a garbage can, dumpster, or recycling bin outside. A collector empties the garbage container into a truck. The truck takes the garbage to a dump or recycling center.

A **dumpster** is large enough to hold all kinds of trash.

A **lifting arm** picks up the heavy dumpster and empties it into the truck.

Inside, a **compactor** squashes the garbage. Now there is room for even more.

It's a fact!

Some garbage can be used again and again. This is called recycling. Old cans can be recycled into new cars!

The compactor pushes the garbage deep into the **hopper**.

At the dump, a garbage truck empties its load. The back of the truck lifts up, and all the garbage tumbles out.

Car transporter

A car transporter is a truck that collects shiny new cars from a factory and delivers them to a store where they are sold. It can carry lots of cars at the same time.

The cars are packed tightly together on the **decks**. This transporter has a top deck and a bottom deck.

Metal **locks** stop the cars from falling off the truck.

A mechanic drives the cars up a short **ramp** onto the car transporter.

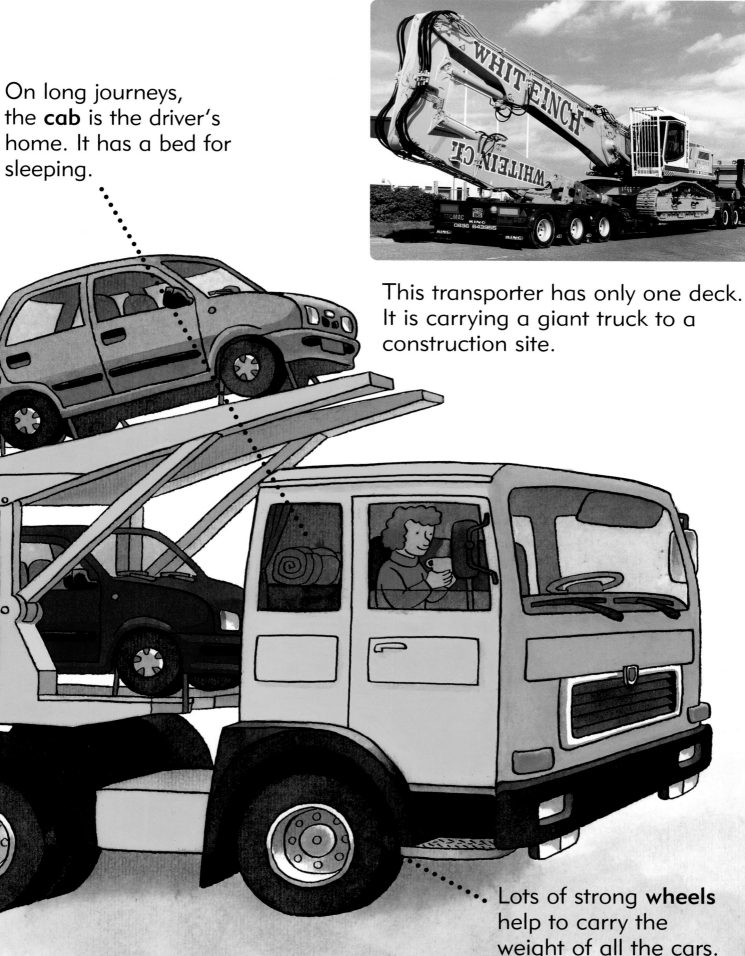

On long journeys, the **cab** is the driver's home. It has a bed for sleeping.

This transporter has only one deck. It is carrying a giant truck to a construction site.

Lots of strong **wheels** help to carry the weight of all the cars.

Fire engine

At the fire station, a loud alarm bell sounds! Within minutes, a shiny red fire engine and its crew arrive at the fire. On board the engine is a hose. The firefighters use it to spray water to put out the fire.

The **ladder** stretches high, so that the firefighter can point the hose at the flames.

A long hose carries water from a **fire hydrant** to the fire.

he firefighter stands
a **safety cage**.

Fireproof clothes keep
the firefighter safe
from the scorching
heat and flames.

Flashing lights and a
loud siren warn people
to stay out of the way.

It's a fact!

Some fire engines carry their own
water. The biggest fire engines hold
enough water to
fill 75 bathtubs!

1

Tractor

On a farm, a tractor helps with lots of jobs all year. It pulls or pushes heavy equipment through fields and over rugged ground. Depending on the season, a farmer may use a tractor to plow a field, cut or carry hay, or even pick fruit.

It's a fact!

The Big Bud 16V 747 tractor has back wheels that are taller than most adults.

This tractor is pulling a trailer. The trailer is piled high with hay for animals.

This tractor is pulling a **plow**. A plow digs up hard soil so that seeds can be planted.

Big side **mirrors** help the driver to see all around the big truck.

A **mudguard** stops mud from splashing into the driver's cab.

Thick tires help the tractor move easily through muddy fields.

23

Around town

Lots of tough trucks are out and about in the slush and snow. They all are doing different jobs.

24

Words you know

Here are some words that you read earlier in this book. Say them out loud, then try to find the things in the picture.

hose

thick tires

blade

ramp

ladder

hopper

Which truck is pushing snow off the road?

25

How many cars are on the decks of the car transporter?

Did you know?

Cement mixers weigh 20,000–30,000 pounds (9–14 metric tons), and can carry about 40,000 pounds (18 metric tons) of concrete.

The British word for truck is *lorry.*

The crane was first used by the ancient Greeks to build temples.

The reason why the rear wheels on tractors are so much bigger than the front wheels is because the big wheels keep the tractor steady. The front wheels are small to make steering easier.

A fire truck's ladder can be raised as high as about eight stories.

The *boom* (long metal arm) on the largest fire trucks can extend 150 feet (46 meters).

Puzzles

Close-up!

We've zoomed in on parts of different trucks. Can you guess which trucks you are looking at?

1

2

3

Answers on page 32.

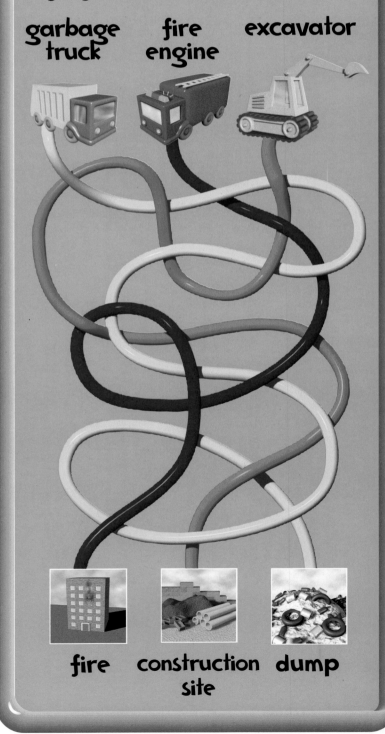

Follow me!

Can you figure out where the garbage truck, fire engine, and excavator are going? Follow the lines to find out!

garbage truck   fire engine   excavator

fire   construction site   dump

Match up!

Match each word on the left with its picture on the right.

1. snowplow

2. tractor

3. cement mixer

4. car transporter

5. crane

6. fire engine

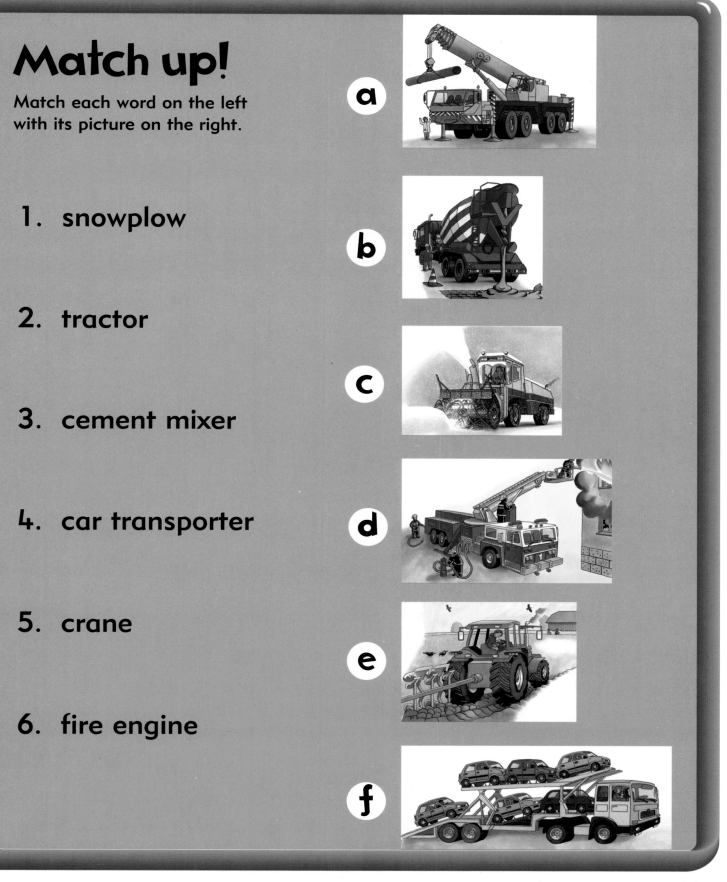

a

b

c

d

e

f

Answers on page 32.

True or false

Can you figure out which of these facts are true? You can go to the page numbers listed to help you find the answers.

The drums of some cement mixers are large enough to hold a car.
Go to page 8.

3

It takes one person 100 days to move as much dirt as an excavator can move in one hour.
Go to page 10.

1

The tractor called Big Bud 16V 747 has tires taller than most adults.
Go to page 22.

4

Old cans can be used to make new cars.
Go to page 17.

2

Some bulldozers can work underwater.
Go to page 5.

5

Answers on page 32.

30

Find out more

Books

Dig Dig Digging, Margaret Mayo (Henry Holt, 2002)
Catchy rhymes introduce you to 11 different kinds of heavy trucks.

Giant Vehicles, Jim Mezzanotte (Gareth Stevens, 2006) 6 volumes
Each book gives lots of facts about one of these vehicles: bulldozers, diggers, dump trucks, loaders, scrapers, and tractors.

Humvees, Janet Piehl (Lerner Publishing Group, 2006)
Discover what a humvee is, with the help of a diagram and glossary.

The Mighty Street Sweeper, Patrick H. Moore (Henry Holt, 2006)
Compared to a bulldozer or grader, the street sweeper isn't very big, but the work it does in your neighborhood is very VERY big.

Monster Trucks, Sarah Levete (Raintree, 2005)
Fact boxes and sidebars add to your knowledge of how big trucks are designed and work.

Websites

How Caterpillar Skid Steer Loaders & Multi Terrain Loaders Work,
How Stuff Works
http://science.howstuffworks.com/skid-steer.htm
Learn how these two types of loaders are used for moving dirt and building materials at construction sites.

How Fire Engines Work, How Stuff Works
http://science.howstuffworks.com/fire-engine.htm
Learn about the main parts of a fire engine, especially the cabin for the firefighters, the toolbox, and the water tank.

Tractor Stories by Kids for Kids, Yesterday's Tractor Co.
http://www.ytmag.com/kstorys.htm
Read what some kids have to say about tractors in this collection of stories by kids from ages four through nine.

Traffic Safety Kids Page, New York State Governor's Traffic Safety Committee
http://www.safeny.ny.gov/kids.htm
Every day you meet cars, trucks, buses, and trains on the road, and this website will teach you how to keep yourself safe around them.

Answers

Puzzles
from pages 28 and 29

Close-up!
1. crane
2. snowplow
3. excavator

Match up!
1. c
2. e
3. b
4. f
5. a
6. d

True or false
from page 30

1. true
2. true
3. false
4. true
5. true

Index